WORKSHY
by Andy Dobb

Published by Playdead Press 2014

© Andy Dobb 2014

Andy Dobb has asserted his rights under the Copyright, Design and Patents Act, 1988, to be identified as the author of this work.

A CIP catalogue record for this book is available from the British Library.

ISBN 978-1-910067-14-7

Caution
All rights whatsoever in this play are strictly reserved and application for performance should be sought through the author before rehearsals begin. No performance may be given unless a license has been obtained.

This book is sold subject to the condition that it shall not by way of trade or otherwise, be lent, resold, hired out, or otherwise circulated without the publisher's prior consent in any form of binding or cover other than that in which it is published and without a similar condition including this condition being imposed on the subsequent purchaser.

Printed by BPUK

Playdead Press
www.playdeadpress.com

Workshy was performed on Wednesday 23rd and Thursday 24th April 2014 at Create Theatre, Mansfield. It was produced as part of Mansfield Palace Theatre's 'Write Track' new writing program and co-produced by Create Theatre, Mansfield, with support from staff and students of Vision West Nottinghamshire College Performing Arts Department.

CAST

JOE	Reece Armstrong
MANDY	Kat Froggatt
BEN	Matt Lamb
HANNAH	Steph Kirk
HARRY	Toby Ryde
RUTH	Hollie Dixon

CREATIVE

Writer	Andy Dobb
Director	Christopher Neil
Dramaturg	Kevin Fegan
Designer	Rebecca Overton
Lighting & Projection	Mark Dimartino Marriott
Producers	Mansfield Palace Theatre & Create Theatre

Andy Dobb | Writer

After securing a BA (Hons) Theatre Arts Degree (First) through Notts Trent Uni (via NCN) in 2007, Andy has been developing his writing skills in conjunction with Kevin Fegan and the Write Tracks group at the Palace Theatre in Mansfield. His short play *Horse to Water* (2008) was developed as part of the first wave of Write Track writers to pass through the Palace and since then he has focused on developing a theatrical voice of his own at a steady pace - making best efforts to balance his working life (performing arts teacher) and personal life (father of four) with his professional desires (writer/actor).

In November 2011 Mansfield Palace Theatre professionally produced *Are You There?* as part of their studio drama commitment to the Write Track group. In 2012 after working on scripts with two Palace Theatre Youth groups, Andy was commissioned to write a new play for 60 young people – *Port Manteau* was performed in February of 2013 on the Palace Theatre main stage. Andy is incredibly grateful for the support and opportunities provided by the Palace Theatre and continues to be an active member of the Write Track group – regularly performing on the script in hand nights where the writers get to share and discuss each other's work with an audience. *Workshy* marks the third time that Mansfield Palace Theatre has engaged and worked with Andy as a writer.

Christopher Neil | Director and Co-Producer

As Education Manager at the Mansfield Palace Theatre, Christopher has encouraged, produced and directed new writing over the past five years. Plays directed include: *Marshmallow Sky* by Alan Dawson, *Are You There?* by Andy Dobb, *Born Thirsty* by Jack Burrows and *In Manifest* by Richard Woodward. For Mansfield Palace Theatre, he also directed *Not Much Matches Mansfield* by Kevin Fegan, a commissioned community play in 2012. Over the past decade, as a freelance director and facilitator, Christopher has worked at new writing festivals including the Write Now Festival, Liverpool and the Manchester 24:7 Festival. Plays directed include: *My Life's Work* by James Allen and Jack Lord, *Under The Dirt* by Claire Berry, and *The Opposite of Claustrophobic* and *Human Habitation* by Rob Johnston. Recent devising / directing work includes *Playful Acts of Rebellion* for The Gramophones Theatre Company.

Kevin Fegan | Dramaturg

Kevin Fegan is a Playwright & Poet. He has written to commission around 50 original plays for a wide variety of theatre, several plays and drama serials for BBC Radio 4 and has worked as a Storyline Writer for Granada TV's *Coronation Street*. Kevin has published 10 collections of poetry. Latest stage plays include *Obama the Mamba* , co-production Curve Leicester & The Lowry Salford (Nominated Best New Play Manchester Theatre Awards 2012, published by Playdead Press); *Slave*, Feelgood Theatre at The Lowry & national tour (Winner Best New Play Manchester Evening News Theatre Awards 2010 and

Winner Best Play or Film Human Trafficking Foundation 2011); *Fireflies: a love story waiting to happen* commissioned & produced by The Lowry (Nominated Best New Play M.E.N. Theatre Awards 2010). www.kevinfegan.co.uk

Mark Dimartino Marriott | Lighting/Projection Design
Mark studied Theatre Arts at the University of Derby where he specialised in Technical Theatre and Design. He likes to work creatively, immersing the audience into the piece through his designs. His work spans many styles of performance and his lighting and sound designs and technical input has featured in both local amateur pieces and touring professional pieces. Mark has a passion for theatre that has led him to work in several venues across the country and with an extensive ranges of theatre companies.

Mansfield Palace Theatre

Under the guidance of local professional playwright, Kevin Fegan, new writing for theatre has been encouraged and developed over several years at the Mansfield Palace Theatre through the Write Track Group, a team of 15 to 20 local playwrights. As part of this work, for the last four years, Mansfield Palace Theatre has annually commissioned one of the group members to write a new play which has been professionally produced.

As *Workshy* focuses on six young people in their teenage years and had already had some early development with performing arts students from Vision West Nottinghamshire College, Mansfield Palace Theatre thought it most appropriate to team up with the College and Create Theatre. This partnership has worked well with the development of new writing in the local Mansfield area also providing the opportunity for six student actors to work in a professional environment, with professional practitioners and to experience a full time rehearsal process.

Mansfield Palace Theatre is delighted to be co-producing *Workshy* and encouraging the development of local artists in Mansfield.

Create Theatre

About Create

Create Theatre has already become one of the leading centres for creative arts in the region. A small-scale venue with large-scale ambition.

Based at Vision West Nottinghamshire College, this 150-seat contemporary performance space offers the best in drama, fringe, stand-up and musical theatre to Mansfield and the surrounding area. We pride ourselves in programming performances that showcase new writing, emerging artists and locally-produced theatre and companies.

Create works closely with the students of West Nottinghamshire, local theatre groups and national touring theatre companies to bring affordable art and entertainment to the town.

More than just a theatre; Create offers facilities and rehearsal space for aspiring actors and musicians, and regularly works within the community to inspire the next generation of theatre-goers.

Known for its friendly welcome and hospitality (and recognised as family-friendly by the Family Arts Campaign), Create's strong team of volunteers are always ready to greet you, and make sure your visit is one to remember.

A Note from the Co-Producer-Create Theatre

As a supporter of arts in the region, this project ticks various boxes for artistic development and involves so many benefitting partners. The fact we are working with Mansfield Palace Theatre and Education Manager Christopher Neil to develop locally-produced theatre, shows both venues' dedication to the cause. We are delighted that the cast of students from Vision West Nottinghamshire College, who call Create 'home' are getting experience of working with arts professionals in a production process. This will no doubt prove to be invaluable in preparing them for the outside arts world after graduating from the college. The fact that we as a college and a commercial theatre can now offer these kinds of projects as a development tool is testament to how far we have come in such a short space of time.

We are also delighted to be staging a play written by tutor, colleague, actor, director and friend- Andy Dobb. We actively programme and support new-writing in the region, and to be staging a local script by a young theatre maker from the area again proves the worth of having such an ethos.

Adam Pownall Create Theatre Co-ordinator

Author's Note

Workshy started life as nothing more than a phrase in my head and a sense that I wanted to write a piece of Youth Theatre that might engage young actors (and hopefully audiences) in themes and characters that resonate with their own hopes and fears. Working in education, I am acutely aware of the pressures facing young people today – not least the idea that at the age of 16 you should know what it is you want to do for the rest of your life and if you get it wrong then... forget it. The idea of what 'getting it wrong' means interested me also, as it seems to suggest there is a right way of doing things and this started to filter in to my research and thinking as the play developed.

In Oct 2012 I spent a day with students from Vision West Nottinghamshire College Performing Arts Department and asked them to improvise and work through a few questions I had, such as where they got their work ethic from or what their expectations of work were... this was invaluable and I have that select group of students to thank for the play you hold in your hands – its humour, doubts, characters and more can be traced back (through my notes) to that very first workshop.

The script was kept ticking over throughout 2013 until September of that year when the Write Track group was asked to submit plays for the 2014 Mansfield Palace Theatre studio production. I put *Workshy* in, not really expecting much to come of it... how wrong I was... The journey since then to produce a First Draft by January 2014, develop the script across two weekends with the cast, director Christopher Neil and Dramaturg Kevin Fegan in February and March 2014 and hand in the Final Rehearsal Draft has been one of great joy and excitement. It's been hard work – but I've learnt so much as a writer that the late nights and long days development have been more than worth it.

The play being performed is a far cry from the 40 odd pages I had in September 2013 – the influence, advice, guidance and hard work of the cast and creative team has helped me to lift the play out of a one room setting and explore the themes with much bigger brush strokes. The play has few answers within it, but then that's life. What I hope is that actors and audiences leave the theatre and talk – talk about the characters and their lives and through this talk about their own lives. Labelling young people as lazy and workshy is to overlook the complexities of the lives they lead and I hope this play goes someway to address this.

Andy Dobb
Playwright

Director's Note

The development and rehearsing of this play, *Workshy* by Andy Dobb, has been a rewarding experience for all involved. Taking on a play about a group of six friends who have just finished their A levels and about to embark on the World of uncertainty called 'the rest of their lives' has proved to be not only extremely thought provoking from a social point of view but equally challenged the views and responses of all involved from the playwright to the actors to the production team. A play that not only takes on such themes as apathy or disillusionment of young people in Britain today, but equally shows the determination of others to succeed through the fear of failure or desire to build the 'ideal life' is one that affects us all. The pressures put on young people by society is at the heart of this play from the behaviour of the generations that have gone before to the attitudes on what is perceived as a respectable way to go about succeeding in life. Our 'cultured society' may have drilled us to follow the road of education, decent job, house, marriage, kids, but in this day and age does it take us so long to get educated and find the job to enable us to afford the rest, that we lose out on the creating a family element altogether? Are we considered to have failed if we do not have a family? Is it so wrong to have a family in our teens and develop a career after? Others are condemned for their failure to even attempt success according to the rules of an 'effective society'. Learned behaviour and attitudes may lead to patterns within families or communities of second or third generation unemployment being the norm. We may condemn or have a stereotypical view of the young person who is asked not to work by their families or chooses not to work because the financial benefits of 'signing on' are actually more rewarding. Where does the responsibility lie for this seemingly 'stuck in a rut' Britain?

Workshy takes on a lot of issues, raises big questions and shows variation in attitude as a result of society. It holds the mirror up to us, but it is done through six ordinary, genuine human beings just trying to make sense of life. Enjoy this insight into their lives.

Christopher Neil
Director

The Published Text of 'Workshy' was made possible by the generosity of several people who contributed to a Kickstarter Campaign designed to raise the necessary funds. As a reward for their support the following deserve to have their names acknowledged below.

To those listed – Thank you! This would not have been possible without your support.

Dawn Hills, Amy Bedford, Tony Hearn, Heloise Harley, Drew Baxter, Richard Coleman, Natalie Dobb, Graham Dobb, Emma Bray, Donna Kirlew, Dean Leivers, Kay Vardy, Kieran George, Alun Jenkins, Jack Burrows, Matt Brooks, Marie Wragg, Phil Green.

For Beavis, Pig, Bear and Le Bitche

Work hard, make mistakes, work harder, live your dreams.

CHARACTERS:

The following are descriptions of the characters when 'in the present' – (characters are also involved in scenes where they are older or younger or represent people in each other's stories).

JOE 18, never worked, not interested in working, in relationship with **MANDY**, just discovered that he will be a Dad.

MANDY 17, in a relationship with **JOE**, pregnant, had a moment with **HARRY** when on a break from **JOE**, planned to go to Uni with **RUTH** her best friend.

HARRY 18, from an affluent family, doesn't worry about money, had a moment with **MANDY**, expected to work in the family business.

BEN 17, recently started working as a 'refuse collector' with his Dad, close to **HANNAH**, gay.

RUTH 17, **MANDY's** best friend, they've planned to do Uni together, has her own life plan.

HANNAH 17, has been working a P/T job whilst studying for her A Levels, can't say no to people, wants to help everyone, closest to **BEN**.

Note:
- A – at the end of the line indicates an interruption by the following line
- A ... is a broken thought, a change in thought

- Any references that can be updated or made relevant to the cultural and/or social experiences of the cast should be encouraged as long as they localise the story and not interrupt the narrative or themes.
- Strong language is utilised throughout to mimic the language of those involved in the original workshops. This can be exorcised / toned down to suit production needs where necessary.

ONE:

JOE with pushchair and sleeping baby stands in the quiet, building himself up to speak. The others take their place in the space waiting. This moment is out of time and place.

JOE:	Terrified…
ALL:	Terrified?
JOE:	If I'm honest. Fuck all we can do though right?
ALL:	Joe!
JOE:	What?
HANNAH:	Pack it in!
JOE:	What?
MANDY:	Language Joe.
JOE:	Fuck that… If I'm telling him… then it's my way… you know… straight from the… what's it… the mouth… the animal what is it?
HARRY:	Dog?
JOE:	No
HARRY:	Bear?
JOE:	Not helping.
ALL:	Its horse!
BEN:	'Straight from the Horse's mouth' is the saying.
HARRY:	Horses can't talk.
BEN:	Neither can dogs and bears.
HARRY:	Bullshit Bennie boy because I've seen one on YouTube, dog, does this thing with its

ALL:	teeth, well funny – (*attempting to imitate the dog*) Rossages...
ALL:	(Laughing) Rossages!
JOE:	Oi! I need to get this right and you lot pissing about is not helping.
MANDY:	Just be honest Joe.
ALL:	Honest?
MANDY:	Yes.
RUTH:	If you'd been more careful Joe then –
MANDY:	What's that supposed to mean?
HANNAH:	Guys!
RUTH:	Well both of you really –
HANNAH:	Go on Joe

(*JOE takes in his surroundings, observing where the others are*)

JOE:	We can start out on the estate, get a house–
RUTH:	Is that what you want Mand? House on Clearview?
BEN:	I live on there
HANNAH:	Me too...
MANDY:	My Grandma did...
HARRY:	Ha! Tramps!
BEN:	Your Dad owns a sock factory, hardly Lord Sugar is he?
HARRY:	It's in the breeding though mate, true story, heard my Dad talk about it in Race Horses. That's what we are – thoroughbred –
ALL:	Stop shooting this down.

JOE:	I'm trying... fuck... at least I'm trying
HANNAH:	We know Joe.
JOE:	What's the fucking point? I've no idea what I was doing before and I've still not got a clue.
ALL:	Try.
JOE:	I know what I'm supposed to say. I'm supposed to say that I'll be there for you, both of you, that I'll go to fucking... work... and start paying for shit, put food on the... but I don't know how to do any of that.
ALL:	You have to try.
JOE:	And my Dad can't say fuck all about any of this cos he's not got a clue... only thing he ever did for me was put a knife to a guys throat when he came round our house shouting about how I'd smashed his garden up... fucking hero... and then he took me in the house and kicked the shit out of me. Is that what I'm supposed to do?
MANDY:	You're not your... it doesn't have to be the same
RUTH:	Will be... living on that estate.
MANDY:	Ruth –
HARRY:	She's right.
BEN:	Two Oaks isn't exactly Buckingham Palace either is it?
HARRY:	Houses cost twice what they do down your end

BEN: Great... so your parents have paid twice as much to live in the same shithole town as the rest of us.

HANNAH: I don't have time for this.

HARRY: You don't have time for anything but frying chicken and homework Nannah.

RUTH: We hardly see you.

BEN: (*To* Ruth) That's not fair.

HANNAH: Look... none of us get it right. Do we?

ALL: No.

HANNAH: What about you Ruth? Where are you going to end up?

RUTH: I've a plan. I'll be where I want to be – Uni, Job, Man, House, Family.

(As RUTH starts to speak, the group pick up her cue and finish her 'mantra' for her)

ALL: Uni, Job, Man, House, Family.

RUTH: Nothing wrong with that. Right way to do it.

HANNAH: Really?

RUTH: (*Not Convincing*) Yes.

HANNAH: Ben? Harry?

BEN: Work hard, make money, move out.

HARRY: On a plate Nannah, on a plate.

ALL: Hang on... What about you Little Superstar/Star Student/Star of the Month?

HANNAH: Me? A Star? No... Far from it...

JOE: So you're all as fucked up as me then?

MANDY: In our own way...
ALL: Yes.
JOE: And look at you... with it all mapped out. The world at your... feet... like that careers twat used to bang on about.
ALL: All mapped out.

(They all take a moment to consider their own lives/journeys)

TWO:

An affluent living room turned upside down by a party. A map has been crudely drawn onto a wall of the house (hidden behind a picture/canvas). It depicts the 'hopes/dreams' of the group of friends. MANDY lies on the sofa sleeping, JOE sits on the edge of one arm of the sofa staring at MANDY. HARRY is prostrate on the floor with RUTH's arm around him. HANNAH is tidying up some of the mess as BEN enters from the kitchen in a rush. BEN searches the room; he has no shirt or shoes on.

BEN:	Fuck. Fucking fuck fuck.
HANNAH:	Try the kitchen.
BEN:	I just did.
HANNAH:	Nothing?
BEN:	What do you think?
JOE:	Alright... keep your shirt on.
BEN:	Prick.

(BEN goes back into the kitchen. JOE strokes MANDY's hair gently. HARRY stirs)

HARRY:	Time?
JOE:	Morning.
HARRY:	Is it light out?
HANNAH:	Yeah... only just.
HARRY:	Shit. Too early. What you doing that for?
HANNAH:	Couldn't leave it a mess.
HARRY:	Nice one Nannah Bananah.

(BEN re-enters the living room)

BEN: H. You haven't seen my shirt and shoes have you?
HARRY: Your... What you looking for?
BEN: My shirt and shoes. I've got half hour to get to work or else I'm fucked. Can't find them anywhere...
HANNAH: They were in your bag, you brought them with you –
HARRY: A blue one?
BEN: Yes, have you seen it?
HARRY: Try the back yard.
BEN: The back... pricks... I'm surrounded by pricks.

(BEN goes into the kitchen again)

JOE: He wishes.
HARRY: All the time... How long you been up?
JOE: Not slept.
HANNAH: Could have helped with the clean up.
JOE: Not my job.
HANNAH: Never is. I'm going to check upstairs...

(HANNAH exits through the Kitchen.)
(A moment)

HARRY: Mad night yeah?
JOE: Yeah.

HARRY:	It's a good job we saved the best party until after all the exams were done... I can only just remember my own name after last night... How come you stayed up? (*Gesturing towards Mandy*) You been in it?
JOE:	No. Things to... talk about.
HARRY:	Talk?
JOE:	(*Distracting*) Someone's written on your Mum's wall.
HARRY:	What? Shit...

(HARRY gets up to inspect the wall)

	Where?
JOE:	There. Behind that picture frame. You can see it sticking out the sides.

(HARRY takes the picture from the wall to reveal a hand drawn 'map'. BEN enters from the garden with a shirt but no shoes on)

BEN:	Why am I out there picking up my clothing from all over your garden.
HARRY:	(*Reading the wall*) What's the... why guys? Why?
BEN:	(*Seeing the Map*) I'd forgot about that.
HARRY:	You did this?
BEN:	No.
HARRY:	Well your fucking name's on here.
JOE:	All our names are on there.

HARRY:	Well who's stupid arse idea was that?
JOE/BEN:	Yours.
HARRY:	No I... (*a beat*) Shit... You might be right.
JOE:	We are.
BEN:	Besides; most of it is in your handwriting.

(HARRY inspects the writing up close)

HARRY:	Shit! I don't need this today.
BEN:	(*Sarcastic*) Ok then... Your minor crisis over?
JOE:	It's only just started by the looks of it.
BEN:	Well put it to one side a minute... two things – why were all my clothes thrown all over the back yard and where are my work boots?
HARRY:	I don't know Bennie Boy... It's not priority number one right now. Mum's going to kill me when she sees this.
JOE:	You've not seen the giant cock on the wall in the bathroom yet then?
HARRY:	Shut up –
JOE:	Suit yourself.

(HARRY runs off through the kitchen to check)

BEN:	Do you know Joe? Why my stuff has been–
JOE:	You emptied your bag out on the yard when you were kicking off about how your

	shit job got in the way of you enjoying yourself.
BEN:	Coming back to me... And the boots?
JOE:	Try the ceiling fan in the kitchen.
BEN:	Pricks...

(HARRY, HANNAH and BEN pass in the kitchen doorway. Exchange of lines as they cross paths)

HARRY:	There's a giant knob in the toilet.
BEN:	Give him my number then.
HARRY:	You're going to tell me I did that too aren't you? Ruth's cocktail idea was wrong, wrong wrong...
HANNAH:	That wasn't you.
HARRY:	Thank fuck –
JOE:	I did that one.
HARRY:	What? Why? You're a complete arsehole Joe. I'm going to have to paint over it.
HANNAH:	He'll scrub it off later... won't you Joe?
JOE:	Yeah... course...
HARRY:	No you won't... you never do... You go round messing up everybody else's shit and then leave them to deal with it.
JOE:	Whatever... Mummy's boy.
HARRY:	Don't start on –

(A noise followed by a cry from the kitchen. BEN re-enters covered in vomit)

JOE:	Find them?
BEN:	Someone. Was. Sick. In. My. Fucking. Boots.
HARRY:	I think it's the shirt you should be more worried about.
BEN:	I thought it might be quicker to turn the light on so the fan would throw them down. I was right.
HARRY:	It smells like Jaeger. Weren't Mandy on that Joe?
JOE:	Not last night, no.
HARRY:	Ruth then?
BEN:	Pricks... I'm going to be late for work now, if I make it in at all.
JOE:	So? Last night you said you didn't care about your shitty job.
BEN:	I don't think any of us were of sound mind last night, do you? I need this job. We can't all sponge of the system for the rest of our lives.
JOE:	Who's a sponge?
HANNAH:	Harry take him upstairs... see if you can find anything.
HARRY:	(*To Ben*) Come on mate
JOE:	(*To Ben*) Who's the sponge?
HANNAH:	(*Exasperated*) I suppose I'll be clearing up that mess too right?
JOE:	(*To Ben*) Who's the fucking sponge? Prick.

(BEN exits with JOE in pursuit)

HARRY: Has anyone ever told you how much of a star you are Nannah? Oi Joe give it a rest!

(HARRY exits)

THREE:

BEN aged 7, playing wrestling with a large teddy bear in his bedroom. He acts out the action.

BEN: (*Imitating a wrestling commentator*) Oh he's got him now, got him on the ropes, it's a one two, one two oh my God he's going for the body slam, it's all over now...

(He picks up the bear and body slams it, he then plays to the 'crowd' listening to them roar).

(*Commentator*) This is it; he's going to the top rope! He's going for the flying elbow drop, his signature move!

(He climbs up onto a chair, poses before jumping on to the bear and slamming an elbow into his throat, before he 'lands' the bear 'rolls' out of the way).

(*Commentator*) Oh my goodness, oh my goodness... he missed, he looks out cold

(A sharp knock on the door, threatening. BEN lies still. HARRY as BEN's Dad speaks from behind the door - offstage)

B/DAD: You jumping around in there?
BEN: No.

B/DAD:	Don't lie to me. Sounded like the kitchen ceiling was falling through. What you playing at?
BEN:	Nothing. I'm just... I was...
B/DAD:	I've told you before about jumping around wrestling... you got your Mum's bear in there as well?
BEN:	No.
B/DAD:	Ben...
BEN:	Yes... Sorry Dad...
B/DAD:	Put it back and get downstairs. Now! It's about time you stopped playing them games.
BEN:	(*Almost sobbing*) Ok...
B/DAD:	When I was your age I was working up the farm with Uncle Jack, not pissing about like them... wrestlers... in their pants.
BEN:	(*Fighting the sobbing*) Ok...
B/DAD:	And stop crying.
BEN:	I'm not.
B/DAD:	Bloody baby. Big bloody baby.

(*The sound of large feet thudding down wooden stairs.*)
(*BEN is fighting the tears back. He picks up the bear but as he goes to move he trips over. He rages and thrashes at the bear, not pretend as before, lashing out in anger, before hugging it tightly. He moves in the space and increases in age. Now 16 he picks up the black bin liner left by Hannah in TWO. He places the bear in it, ties it up and throws it over his shoulder with a whistle.*)

FOUR:

Late at night, a high street, *HANNAH rushes across the space. The rest of the cast in the shadows call out obscenities - like drunken animals – they bark orders for food, they wolf whistle, sexist comments, football chants. It is the noise of the weekend. HANNAH is scared. HANNAH runs from the barking straight into BEN who has come to pick her up.*

BEN: Nannah!? You ok? You sounded weirded out on the phone –
HANNAH: I'm fine. Extra shift –
BEN: Again?
HANNAH: Yeah it's fine. Just didn't fancy walking through town –
BEN: No. Of course...
HANNAH: Sorry to text you so late. I didn't... I just thought you'd be up.
BEN: I was. Will be for a bit yet. You look terrified –
HANNAH: (*Changing the subject*) I just didn't fancy getting the bus on my own. Not tonight.
BEN: You going home?
HANNAH: Is that ok?
BEN: Whatever you need. Dad would probably shit the bed if he saw me walking in with a girl 'after hours'...
HANNAH: You're a star Ben. A star.
BEN: I have my moments

(*They stand waiting for a bus, Hannah exhausted yet on edge*)

HANNAH: Sorry about this.
BEN: Stop apologising, it's getting embarrassing.
HANNAH: Sorry... Mum's too ill to come out so...
BEN: Hannah... its fine...

(*A moment*)

    They change your shift again?
HANNAH: Sort of.
BEN: Pricks.
HANNAH: My fault really. I could have turned them down
BEN: But you 'need' the money?
HANNAH: Something like that.
BEN: You know I thought working would be a bit more... not glamorous... but –
HANNAH: Respectable?
BEN: God no! If I'm ever that I give you permission to take me out back and shoot me.
HANNAH: What then?
BEN: I don't know... just... better I suppose. I mean... having money in your pocket... that feels good... but... I don't know.
HANNAH: I know what you mean.
BEN: Look at us. You fry chicken and walk the streets late at night, whilst I get up at the

	crack of dawn and shovel other people's shit around...
HANNAH:	At least we're earning something... I can't imagine what Mand and Joe are going through at the minute.
BEN:	(*Fondly*) Yeah. Pricks.
HANNAH:	I couldn't do it. Having something rely on you... completely. Terrifying.
BEN:	Like I said – Pricks!
HANNAH:	You can't say that.
BEN:	Look Joe is one of my oldest friends. I love him to bits. But he's not up to it.
HANNAH:	He might surprise us.
BEN:	Alright Little Miss Glass-Half Full.
HANNAH:	He might. Could be what he needs.
BEN:	What he needs is a rocket up his arse.
HANNAH:	Not a prick then?
BEN:	(*Sarcastic*) Ha Ha...
HANNAH:	Your trouble is you can give it but you can't take it Ben.
BEN:	Alright enough... I expect this kind of abuse from H...

(*A moment as they share each other's company*)

HANNAH:	Well I think they'll be alright. They'll sort it.
BEN:	We'll see.
HANNAH:	They've got to be...

(*A moment*)

	I'm back here again at 11am for the change over.
BEN:	You're doing too much you.
HANNAH:	I'm not guaranteed work on this zero hours contract, feels like I should take it when I can.
BEN:	The hours you're putting in they'll be making you management by the end of the month.
HANNAH:	Great! I can go from frying chicken to watching others fry chicken.
BEN:	Sounds very 'respectable'.
HANNAH:	Shut up...

(*HANNAH and BEN wait for the bus in silence. Blackout*)

FIVE:

(HANNAH addresses the audience)

HANNAH: I've always found it hard to say no. It used to annoy me when I was a kid because it meant... I never got what I wanted. I tried to say it more as I grew up... realised that I was always being walked on... over... but... it's not me, not my nature. So in the end I thought I'd just... you know... accept it. Which makes life... complicated... sometimes...

(RUTH and MANDY enter to play out the other voices. Performed with an exaggerated sense of intensity)

BOSS:	Hannah – glad I caught you... There's an extra shift come up if you want it?
HANNAH:	What day?
TUTOR:	Hannah can I just have a word.
BOSS:	Tomorrow
HANNAH:	(*To* Tutor) I'm just off to –
TUTOR:	It won't take a minute.
HANNAH:	Right... (*To Boss*) I'm already working the morning...
BOSS:	I know that. I'm short staffed.
HANNAH:	Can I even do a double shift?
BOSS:	No problem.

TUTOR: We need someone to show new students round, we can't think of anyone better to do the job. You up for it?

HANNAH: (*To* Tutor) When is it?

TUTOR: Tomorrow evening.

HANNAH: (To *Boss*) *W*e do have this open evening coming up and I've been asked to... but I guess I could –

BOSS: If I need to send anyone home early then I'll put you top of the list, hey?

HANNAH: (*To Tutor*) It's our half-day tomorrow I've agreed to go to work 12 – 4 and then I've got to go back for 8 – 12.

TUTOR: It would be a massive help if you could?

BOSS: How's that? Hannah? If I put you top of the list?

TUTOR: This would only be for half an hour, 6:30 – 7pm.

HANNAH: (*To* Both) Ok... why not.

BOSS: Brilliant – you're a star Hannah!

TUTOR: You're a star Hannah! An absolute star! See you at 6.

HANNAH: You're a star... Stupid saying really. People like me, the 'stars' of this world, we usually spend our time running round after others. But that's not what *stars* do. *Stars* are the centre... the force of gravity comes from... is formed by...

(*A moment*)

Sometimes I can see myself as all that. But then other times... What I fear the most is what happens when a star... dies out... explodes... implodes... burns so hot that it shrinks... down... then black hole... sucking everything in... yeah... I fear that the most.

(*HANNAH is lost in this thought for a brief moment.*)

SIX:

Six months after the party in TWO. MANDY and JOE in MANDY's Mum's house, sparse. Wrapped in blankets against the cold, they've obviously been sleeping on the sofa. JOE watches MANDY sleeping. She wakes.

MANDY:	Do you sit watching me sleep every night?
JOE:	How you feeling?
MANDY:	I've just woken up Joe, give me a minute.
JOE:	But its morning. Don't you need to... you know –

(JOE mimes being sick)

MANDY:	I don't think it works like that.
JOE:	Right.
MANDY:	Has everyone gone?
JOE:	Your Mum left an hour ago, must be mad going up that hill to clean school toilets in this weather.
MANDY:	It's only rain
JOE:	It's pissing it down! I've been watching the trees over the road, thought they were going to snap in two.
MANDY:	You're such a drama queen
JOE:	You shouldn't say things like that.
MANDY:	Why?
JOE:	Because it hurts... (*Touching his heart, mock sincerity*) right here.

MANDY: (*Mocking further* still) Poor little man
JOE: (*Rolling up his sleeves, Playful*) Right that's it.
MANDY: You think you've got a chance?
JOE: You won't know what's hit you

(*JOE starts to tickle MANDY*)

MANDY: No Joe don't not with this lump
JOE: Too late, should have thought about that before

(*JOE tickles MANDY again, playful – she screams and struggles as they giggle together*)

MANDY: Stop it, stop it... the bump...
JOE: Oh yeah using kid as an excuse already
MANDY: Help us up, I need to get up.

(*JOE helps MANDY to sit up*)

JOE: Don't get used to this.

(*A moment where their childish game meets the reality of her physical situation*)

MANDY: I've got the hospital later...
JOE: I'll come with you.
MANDY: You don't have to... (*a beat*) I think Mum wants to come. If she can get...

JOE:	But I want to go. It's what I should be doing isn't it?
MANDY:	Joe...
JOE:	Yeah yeah... save it...
MANDY:	We're lucky she understands... starting to become a bit of a family tradition really.
JOE:	I know –
MANDY:	I don't think she expected me to... but now that we're... it's on its way... I'm kind of glad she's been where we are now.
JOE:	It's alright for you. You didn't get the bollocking I got.
MANDY:	She had to get it out her system somehow. She's fine with you now.
JOE:	I thought she was going to stab me with that spoon Mand, it wasn't funny.
MANDY:	Me and Ruth thought it was.
JOE:	Mand...
MANDY:	A little bit?
JOE:	I'm just glad your Dad's not around... it was bad enough telling mine.

(A beat.)
(The moment shifts a little)

MANDY:	This baby... our baby... its –
JOE:	A mistake?
MANDY:	Not what we planned.
JOE:	I've never planned for anything.
MANDY:	We can't do this alone –

JOE: Look... I know this baby is just something else I'm expected to fuck up completely like everything else... but I want to try... honest –

MANDY: Oh I feel sick

JOE: Thanks! I thought I was being –

MANDY: No I mean... I told you not to be rough... I actually feel sick... I think I need to...

(*MANDY rushes off to the toilet. JOE sits and listens to the not too distant sound of MANDY being sick. The weight of his situation plays out a moment*)

SEVEN:

JOE is returning from a job interview. JOE was late and has been rejected. The others wait for him, they carry items of clothing to dress him in. This is out of space/time.

JOE:	I was late. It was... the bus driver...
ALL:	Late? Again?
HARRY:	And how are you dressed?
JOE:	What?
BEN:	You can't go for an interview in jeans and converse mate.
HARRY:	Especially if they've not been washed for weeks.

(HARRY comes forward with a paisley shirt)

> You can borrow one of my Dad's shirts if you like.

(They all look at the shirt and start to giggle)

JOE:	What's that?
HARRY:	What's wrong with it? My Dad knows what to wear at interviews and stuff.

(They giggle some more)

> What?

BEN:	All I'm saying is that I'm gay and I wouldn't wear that mate.
HARRY:	Floral shirts aren't gay. My Dad wears them all the time.
ALL:	Whilst he's out dogging?
HARRY:	My Dad doesn't go...
JOE:	Did you just say Floral?
ALL:	He did.
HARRY:	Oi what is this? I'm trying to help you out you bastard. It's what my Dad calls them. They're floral patterns, paisley, and it's a Ben Sherman so don't go fucking it up with... stains...
JOE:	I won't have it out, believe me. I'll keep my jacket on.

(*JOE strips off and HARRY puts the shirt on him. JOE stands with nothing but the shirt on waiting for the next 'bright' idea*)

MANDY:	You need to borrow a suit.
JOE:	Why? It won't make any difference.
ALL:	At the minute it would.
HARRY:	(*Pointing to JOE in his pants*) Is it cold in here?
JOE:	Funny...
BEN:	Look I wore a suit to my interview
HANNAH:	I went smart-casual.
MANDY:	See? They got the job so... Here – try this.

(*MANDY dresses him in the trousers*)

BEN: Shoes mate... here you can have these. As long as I get them back for work.

(*BEN presents JOE with some shiny black leather boots. He replaces JOE's knackered trainers*)

JOE: These are your work boots?
BEN: Yes. New ones... had to replace them after the... incident with the vomit.
JOE: Shiny... Why do you polish them? They must get covered in shit every time you go out.
BEN: Pride. Job satisfaction. Dad's philosophy really. However – I can see his point.
RUTH: (*To* Ben) You are wasted on –
BEN: Save the arguments, I've been over them a million times. I'm not interested. End of.
HARRY: Besides he needs to prove to his old man that he's not a 'softy'.
BEN: Piss off.

(*HANNAH steps forward with a comb.*)

HANNAH: Hat off. Hair –
JOE: It doesn't do anything but this.
HANNAH: Right... just keep the hat off then... and blame it on the wind maybe? Or the bus driver?

MANDY:	You look nice Joe.
ALL:	Yeah. All ready for court.
MANDY:	Give him a break.
HANNAH:	Remember – give eye contact but don't come across as a psychopath.
BEN:	It's best if you give a firm handshake –
HARRY:	(*Innuendo*) I bet it is!
BEN:	(*Ignoring* him) It's a sign of confidence
MANDY:	Have a few questions ready to ask... just in case.
HANNAH:	You don't want to go on and on about nothing
RUTH:	Keep it short and sweet –
HARRY:	Isn't that how he got you pregnant Mand?
BEN:	I heard that was more your style mate?

(*HARRY, unsure, stays quiet*)

RUTH:	(*Smelling at his clothes/trainers*) He stinks.

(*Ruth sprays him with perfume*)

HANNAH:	Not too much of that – might trigger an allergy
HARRY:	Or just smell worse than the BO.
MANDY:	Get there on time for this one.
HANNAH:	Take an earlier bus.
BEN:	Don't lie about your work history
HARRY:	Won't be hard.

BEN:	But make sure you talk about the positives of your time since school.
HANNAH:	Anything you've done for the Jobcentre or at home.
RUTH:	But don't mention sitting on your arse playing Xbox.
ALL:	And don't forget to –

(*JOE has had enough, he is more confused and uncomfortable than before they started*)

JOE:	ARE YOU FUCKING KIDDING ME? LEAVE ME ALONE!
MANDY:	Joe?
JOE:	Look I appreciate the help but... it's not help when it's an overload of do's and don'ts. I'm shit at all this as it is.
HANNAH:	You're right... Just relax. Be yourself.
JOE:	That's the problem. That's the fucking problem right there. I best get gone... thanks... for the...
MANDY:	I'll see you when you get back.
HANNAH:	Good luck.
ALL:	Good luck

(*MANDY kisses him on the cheek. The others wish him good luck in their own way. Eventually JOE stands alone, his old clothes in a pile on the floor beside him.*)

JOE: 167. That's the magic number. 167 rejections. Everything from Catering to Sales Assistant. Everyone of them... a big, fat, no... 167...

(*HARRY, RUTH, BEN, HANNAH remain in the shadows to play out the parts of Interviewers/Jobcentre Workers*)

INTERVIEW1: 'Sorry not enough experience'
INTERVIEW2: 'We're really looking for someone with experience'
INTERVIEW3: 'Have you ever done this sort of work before? No? Primarily we're looking for someone who has, but we'll keep you on file'.
JOE: Bullshit. No one ever calls back. But I'm supposed to... to follow up. Second slap of rejection and embarrassment, as if the looks when I was in the interview didn't say it all.
INTERVIEW1: 'We don't usually give feedback'
INTERVIEW2: 'You were late'
INTERVIEW3: 'You didn't seem interested in the post'
INTERVIEW1: 'You should think about how important first impressions are'
INTERVIEW3: 'Clothes'
INTERVIEW2: 'GCSE Results'
INTERVIEW3: 'Found someone else better suited'
INTERVIEW1: 'Hope this helps you in the future'
JOE: WASTE. OF. SPACE. 167. My magic number.

(*JOE begins to change back into his own clothes as he speaks.*)

                  After the last one I stopped looking. Not worth it. Soon as I was old enough to sign on... I did. They were too busy to give a fuck as well. I used to go in to sign on and write out my Mum's shopping list on my 'evidence' form.

JC/WORKER: 'What have you done to look for work the last two weeks Joe?'

JOE: 'Well... Weetabix, toilet roll and fanny plasters... sorry Sanitary Towels.'

JC/WORKER: 'All looks in order Joe, we'll see you next time'.

JOE: Don't blame them for giving up on me. There's another 6 wasters like me to see that hour and after 167 stabs at it you'd think something would have landed.

(*JOE is now fully dressed in his own clothes. He holds the suit/shirt/boots in a pile*)

                  I thought about the Army. Tried running for a week... you know, training... Wasn't for me.

(*A moment*)

                  167 was the magic number alright. After the last interview was over I only had enough money to get me half way home.

Had to walk the rest of the way. It was raining and I remember crossing every road without looking to see what was coming. Felt like the right thing to do at the time.

(BEN enters with the bin liner again, whistling. JOE throws the suit and shirt in. BEN fishes out the boots, tuts, wraps the bag over his shoulder and whistles a tune.)

EIGHT:

HANNAH at work – a fast food, fried chicken outlet – JOE enters in uniform also, ready to do some training during a busy Saturday lunch period. MIKE (the manager) played by HARRY stands watching them.

HANNAH:	I agree with you.
JOE:	So why do they have it there then?
HANNAH:	Hygiene is important. We're dealing with a high volume of raw and cooked product and customers who pass over money, sneezes, coughs... it's a priority so they make a big deal of it. So – have *you* washed your hands?
JOE:	Yes. Nearly scrubbed my skin off.
HANNAH:	Put these on.

(*HANNAH hands JOE some gloves*)

JOE:	You're kidding?
HANNAH:	Afraid not.
JOE:	This is getting more hassle than it's worth. I already look a dickhead in this uniform.
HANNAH:	Stop complaining, you've only been here an hour. I know it's only a trial, but I'll split my wages for today with you –
JOE:	You can't do –
HANNAH:	Yes I can. If it helps you keep your mind on why your here then I will. I had to

	practically beg Mike to let you do this so... you know... don't let me down.
JOE:	I know... I know... look I'm doing my best and I do you know... what's it... I'm happy that you... that's not it –
HANNAH:	Appreciate.
JOE:	That's it. I appreciate what you're doing. No one else has stuck their neck out for me. You're a star Nannah.
HANNAH:	Come on, let's get you on the tills.

(*HANNAH and JOE go through a rhythm of taking the order, taking the cash, giving the change and so on. This could be pantomime fast or slow motion. Throughout the rest of the cast call out the orders, different voices, different requests. JOE is steadily unnerved by it all*)

JOE:	Is it break yet?
HANNAH:	You're kidding aren't you, it's only been 15min. This is Saturday lunch – we call it the mad hour, because you have to be mad to work it!
JOE:	Shit.

(*Repeat of the pantomime above – even faster/slower than before. The dialogue fires out over the top, sentences not quite finishing before moving on to the next order/voice*)

| **JOE:** | Oh bollocks |

(*MIKE moves as if he is going to intervene, but doesn't*)

HANNAH: (*Noticing Mike*) Not on the shop floor Joe. What is it.
JOE: That last guy... I thought he gave me a £20... I gave him change for a £20... But now I think it was a £10...
HANNAH: Well we can't take your till off at peak time to check... will have to check it when it's quieter. Just keep going.
JOE: What will happen –
HANNAH: Just serve Joe!

(*Repeat of the pantomime above – even faster/slower than before. The dialogue fires out more ferocious, almost as animalistic*)

JOE: FUCKING HELL!

(*MIKE moves as if he is going to intervene again, but doesn't*)

HANNAH: Joe you can't –
JOE: Fuck this Hannah, I'm sorry but fuck this.
HANNAH: Calm down, what is it?
JOE: I've just given that woman <u>his</u> meal, I've ordered two of the wrong thing and my legs are fucking killing me.

(*A beat*)

HANNAH: We've only been on shop floor and hour.

JOE: Exactly... fuck this. I'm out. I can't do it. You're better at this stuff than I am Nannah, sorry. If I don't go then I'm going to end up hitting something... or someone...

HANNAH: Joe...

(JOE storms off, HANNAH is left dumbstruck. MIKE goes to intervene but it is too late. Instead he throws HANNAH a look of displeasure. HANNAH is unnerved by this)

Yes madam? Can I take your order please?

(Lights fade to her light and then to black)

NINE:

MANDY and RUTH at MANDY's house two nights before the party in TWO. Piles of notes and scribbles on scrap paper falling from a notebook, a laptop is open. RUTH is searching for Uni accommodation on the laptop a little flustered. MANDY, upset, has just told RUTH she is pregnant.

RUTH: This could be alright; it's in our budget and it has three rooms... so you know... or maybe –
MANDY: Yeah...
RUTH: Actually – thought – Is Joe planning to stay over?
MANDY: We've not really talked about it... didn't you hear what I just said?
RUTH: Yes.
MANDY: Then why are you carrying on as though you haven't?

(*A moment*)

RUTH: I'm sorry. You caught me off... whatsit... I didn't expect you to just blurt it out. I'm sorry. Are you ok?

(*RUTH gets up to comfort MANDY*)

MANDY: I don't know.
RUTH: What did Joe say?

MANDY: Nothing much... just kept rubbing his head and swearing under his breath.

(*A moment*)

RUTH: So... what's next?
MANDY: I... Well I need to tell Mum.
RUTH: Do you want me to help?
MANDY: No... I think that ones for me and Joe.

(*A moment*)

RUTH: Bloody hell... I'm talking to a Mummy!
MANDY: I've not figured it out completely yet.
RUTH: Well you've 9 months until he/she gets here... That's near enough the first semester at Uni. Then there's Joe or a nursery –
MANDY: Ruth don't.

(*A moment*)

RUTH: Oh you're thinking of –
MANDY: No! Couldn't... we didn't even discuss... that...
RUTH: (*Supportive*) I don't think I could either.
MANDY: I'm sorry. We had plans, I know –
RUTH: Don't be daft! You've got to... do... you know... I mean so what if it's not the 'right way' –
MANDY: Right way?

RUTH: You're about 15yrs too young really –
MANDY: My Mum had me at my age...
RUTH: Shit no... I didn't mean... I just... look you know we've always talked about doing things... a particular way.
BOTH: (*Softly*) Uni, Job, Man, House, Family
RUTH: Maybe you'll just... do it in reverse order?
MANDY: I think man comes before baby? That's pretty much how I remember it.

(*A moment*)

RUTH: And you're sure it's his, Joe's I mean?
MANDY: Ruth!
RUTH: Because the other month you –
MANDY: (*Not convincing*) I'm... sure.
RUTH: Ok

(*A moment*)
(*MANDY has been hurt by RUTH's words*)

MANDY: I can't believe you'd bring that up Ruth.
RUTH: What? It's true though... it's possible isn't it?
MANDY: It's definitely Joe's.
RUTH: Not even a slim chance for Harry then –
MANDY: That was a mistake. One off.
RUTH: Not even if you know his Mum would go crazy over it and buy you all sorts of stuff?

	Probably look after it too, let you go to Uni – well a local one, but still.
MANDY:	No. It's not his. It's Joes. You shouldn't have said anything about Harry. You can't tell him –
RUTH:	What do you take me for?
MANDY:	This is messed up as it is. I don't need him poking his nose into it.
RUTH:	Fine. As long as you're sure.

(*A moment*)

RUTH:	A mummy...
MANDY:	Yeah... a mum...

(*A moment*)

	Actually... Will you come with me... to tell my mum? She might kill Joe if I take him in straight away.
RUTH:	Yeah 'course. What right now?
MANDY:	I think so. Whilst I'm... up for it.
RUTH:	Yeah... I'll just shut this down, tidy up.
MANDY:	I'm just going to... wash my face. Bloody mascara everywhere.
RUTH:	Ok.

(*MANDY leaves the room. A moment as RUTH takes in the laptop and notes/plans for Uni around her. RUTH closes the laptop down and packs things away. RUTH picks up a notebook, it has a picture of her and MANDY on the front. RUTH stuffs other notes and bits of paper into it. BEN enters with the bin bag whistling. BEN offers it to RUTH to put her notebook in. RUTH hesitates but refuses. BEN leaves with a shrug and a whistle.)*

TEN:

RUTH reading her personal statement to a careers tutor. BEN plays the careers tutor.

RUTH: '... in short I think I would be an asset to your course and I'm motivated to start my future with you.'

(*A brief pause as RUTH awaits a response*)

                    Is that alright?
CAREERS: It's alright.
RUTH: Alright??
CAREERS: It's good. Positive and ticks most of the boxes.
RUTH: How do I make it better?
CAREERS: You're missing a little passion
RUTH: Passion? You said not to over complicate things, just get to the point. You said Unis read thousands of these every –
CAREERS: They do. So yours has to stand out.
RUTH: How?
CAREERS: Why do you want to go to Uni?
RUTH: Why?
CAREERS: Yes, why? Your very good at saying what you expect to get from going, which they already know – they wrote their courses, wrote their perspectives, answered your questions on open days... they know all

	that. What they don't know is – why you want to carry on studying?
RUTH:	It's what you do... right?
CAREERS:	Not everyone. So why do you?

(*A beat as RUTH struggles for an answer*)

RUTH:	I've... always enjoyed school, didn't want to leave Primary at first because it was so... and then we came up here on a class visit and I saw the science labs and sports hall and humanities block and... I like to read.
CAREERS:	Go on.
RUTH:	I've always got a book to read, mostly fiction but I read other things too.
CAREERS:	You're getting it – it's not riveting stuff but you're closer to the truth now. Why History?
RUTH:	I've always had a passion for history –
CAREERS:	No! Don't say the word passion! And always? You're 17 you've only been studying it the last 5yrs, you can't have always had a passion –
RUTH:	I used to sit with my Mum and Dad and watch documentaries when I was little. My Mum bought me books from the library about Egypt and Vikings – I love the Vikings. They took me to Yorvik and I... I remember thinking how great it would be to dig up a piece of history from the ground.

	A coin or a shoe… all the stories they could tell, the answers they could give.
CAREERS:	That's better, if you can link it to experiences or extra-curricular activities then it makes your application stronger.
RUTH:	Like doing my work experience at the Museum?
CAREERS:	You did that?
RUTH:	Yes.
CAREER:	That should be in there!
RUTH:	It is. I just didn't think it was academic enough to talk loads about.
CAREER:	You're fighting for a place on a course against hundreds, thousands of people. I'm reading all of these statements and I'm looking for the one… the one that stops me skimming through and actually makes me read it. You've the world at your feet Ruth… fight for your piece of it. Ok? Take that back with you – inject a little passion into it, not too much, just enough to say why you want to carry on studying, what inspires you, what experiences you've had. Do that and you'll be on to a winner.

(*RUTH fiddles with her statement a moment and gets up to leave*)

RUTH:	Thanks… for looking at my statement… I think I know what you mean.

CAREER: You do. Trust yourself. Bring it me back later if you like. Get it right before it goes.
RUTH: Ok.

(*RUTH turns to go*)

CAREERS: Remember! Passion! Sell yourself! You've the world at your feet!

(*RUTH leaves the meeting*)

ELEVEN:

HARRY's house after the party in TWO. Everyone except HANNAH is present and in the middle of a heated discussion

HARRY:	(*Irate*) I don't rely on others to get on mate.
BEN:	You not taking up Mummy and Daddy's offer of a job then?
HARRY:	That's different.
BEN:	How?
HARRY:	Because... if...
JOE:	Not a clue.
HARRY:	Piss off. It's different because they won't let me get away with sitting on my arse. They've never sat on their arses, they've always had to '*work and sacrifice things*'. (*To Ben*) You know what it's like working with family.
BEN:	Yeah... but my Dad isn't my boss. If I get fired I've got to face my Dad knowing I've screwed up.
MANDY:	Shouldn't you be at work now?
RUTH:	Wasn't Hannah your lift in because she left ages ago?
BEN:	Yes thanks, trying to forget that...
RUTH:	None of you have worked as hard as me and Mand. We've given up loads for exams and its all for nothing.
BEN:	(*Sarcastic*) Nothing? Thought you were off to Uni?

RUTH:	I am... I mean... we are. It's just –
MANDY:	We all know people who've, you know, been to Uni but done nothing with their degree, makes you think about whether it's the right thing or not.
RUTH:	(*Challenging Mandy*) It is the right –
HARRY:	(*Pressuring* Mandy) I thought you were all for it?
MANDY:	I am.
HARRY:	You've done nothing but bang on about it the last few months.
MANDY:	Getting a degree is... can be better than not getting one... but Ben's right, there are other –
RUTH:	Going to Uni is still the right thing to do though – Uni, Job, Man, House, Family

(*As usual they all join in for RUTH's mantra*)

ALL:	Uni, Job, Man, House, Family!
BEN:	Right thing? What's wrong with getting a job?
RUTH:	On the bins?
BEN:	Yes on the bins. Will you stop saying it like that?
RUTH:	I'm sorry Ben but I think it's a waste. You should be off to Uni somewhere.
BEN:	In a couple of years I'll have a deposit for a house.
HARRY:	That's bollocks.

BEN: I will. Worked it out with my Dad, they're not fleecing me for board so that I can save to move out. I won't be on the bins forever, probably get promoted in a few years, do something else.

JOE: Can you do that?

BEN: Probably.

HARRY: Not if you get fired today though hey?

MANDY: That sounds pretty good actually Ben.

RUTH: Its sounds like a waste –

BEN: Uni is not for me. Not interested. Sorry.

JOE: I'd like to do something like that.

HARRY: What?

JOE: Job like Ben's and then... promotion... or –

HARRY: You won't mate.

MANDY: He might.

HARRY: This is Joe we're talking about?

MANDY: Why are you being so harsh on him?

JOE: Leave it Mand.

MANDY: Why are you bothered about what Joe does or doesn't do?

HARRY: Mand... I'm sorry... but are you talking about the same guy you dumped the other month because he's done nothing to support you for the last two years

ALL: Harry!

JOE: You're a knob head Harry.

HARRY: Am I?

MANDY: Why did you have to bring that up?

BEN: Bang out of order H.

HARRY:	It's true though. No point denying it….
MANDY:	People change.
HARRY:	Not Joe. Sorry mate but you've been a lazy workshy bastard since the day I met you, it's part of your charm, nothing going to change that.
RUTH:	He doesn't have a choice remember?
MANDY/JOE:	Ruth –

(A beat)

(JOE and MANDY realise they've jumped down RUTH's neck with a little too much vigour and it has been noticed)

BEN:	Why did you just do that?
MANDY:	Just drop it alright.
HARRY:	(*Knowingly*) Why *did* they do that Ruth?
RUTH:	Don't Harry…
HARRY:	No come on. They've spent all night talking instead of partying, Joe's been jumping down your neck every chance he gets… seems odd to me…
MANDY:	Ruth you didn't…
BEN:	Am I missing something?
RUTH:	Look. I…
MANDY:	Why would you… why say anything?
HARRY:	She had to.
JOE:	Fucks sake…
BEN:	Seriously what is it? What did I miss?
HARRY:	Mandy's having a kid.

JOE:	(*To Ruth*) Couldn't help yourself could you?
BEN:	What? Joe's having a kid?
HARRY:	(*Staring at* MANDY) Mandy is.
BEN:	How long?
RUTH:	About two months.
MANDY:	(*Aware of* HARRY) Thanks Ruth. I think you've said enough.
BEN:	Joe's having a kid? That's...
HARRY:	Two months? Mandy? Two months?
MANDY:	Yes.
JOE:	Two months, yes Harry. You got the picture yet?
HARRY:	I'm getting it.
BEN:	Are you... you know... getting rid of it?
MAND:	(*Upset*) Oh God...

(MANDY goes out through the kitchen)

JOE:	(*To RUTH*) Happy now?
RUTH:	No Joe I'm not happy. I'm not happy at all.

(RUTH follows after MANDY. The three boys stand a moment HARRY and JOE frozen by the moment).

BEN:	Fucking hell.

TWELVE:

RUTH a month after the party in TWO. She is packing her things into boxes ready for the move to Uni. Although we are in RUTH's room, MANDY enters another part of the space with her pregnancy showing, dialling on her phone. She is calling RUTH from the hospital. RUTH ignores the call and lets it ring out. MANDY is not surprised. She holds out a picture of the scan she has just had and takes a picture with her phone. She sends this to RUTH. RUTH receives the picture. Stops in her tracks. Tries to ignore it but picks up her phone and calls MANDY back.

MANDY:	Did you get it?
RUTH:	Yeah. What is it?
MANDY:	Don't know yet. You don't find out until the next one.
RUTH:	Right...
MANDY:	Are you busy?
RUTH:	A bit. Packing
MANDY:	Oh God its next week right?
RUTH:	Yes. Mum and Dad are taking me over Saturday morning. Get keys to my room in Halls 10:30, moved in by lunch and then a tour round... sorry you don't want to know –
MANDY:	No it's ok... I do. Are you still doing the Comic Book Themed Fresher's Ball?
RUTH:	We've had our costumes sorted since we sent off UCAS.

MANDY: You can take mine with you if you like... see if someone else... needs... you know.

(*A beat*)

RUTH: Keep it. We can wear them I'm back for Christmas.
MANDY: Doubt it. I'll be massive by then.
RUTH: Yeah, course, stupid...
MANDY: I better go. You're busy and I need to find Joe and the taxi.
RUTH: Sounds like fun.

(*A moment*)
(*This is their 'goodbye'*)

MANDY: I probably won't see you –
RUTH: No probably not, got to go round family before Sat, but if I get chance then –
MANDY: That would be good.
RUTH: Yeah...
MANDY: Bye Ruthy... I love you.
RUTH: You too.
MANDY: Have fun for both of us? Yeah?
RUTH: Yeah. Bye.

(*RUTH hangs up. Both girls stand for a moment and realise just how different their paths have become. MANDY is greeted by JOE who leads her off to the taxi as RUTH continues to pack her things*)

THIRTEEN:

HARRY's house, morning after the party. JOE and HARRY posturing outside away from the others.

HARRY:	Two months?
JOE:	She didn't want to say anything.
HARRY:	How long have you known?
JOE:	Day one.
HARRY:	Does she... know... who...?
JOE:	Fuck you. For even saying that.
HARRY:	You. Of course. Obvious.
JOE:	It is.

(*A moment*)

HARRY:	But it could be...
JOE:	Forget about it mate, not your problem.
HARRY:	I know we've talked about... what happened when –
JOE:	No point. Done with.
HARRY:	You can't be like that. Not now.
JOE:	I can now.
HARRY:	Shit...
JOE:	I'm going to be a part of its life and –
HARRY:	Woah hang on a minute! Jesus...
JOE:	I am.
HARRY:	Look the timing of it all fits... Joe, you can't ignore that.

JOE: We didn't talk about... you and... she asked me not too. Didn't want me doing something I'd regret... but if you keep fucking banging on about this... you need to forget about it.

HARRY: (*To himself*) Shit. Shit. Shit.

(*HARRY stalks the room a little*)
(*A moment*)

We were just pissing about.

JOE: I said –

HARRY: I didn't even think she'd go for it. I was just... showing off and... banter and... you two had split up, again, because you weren't giving her any attention and so I did...

JOE: Gave her more than a little attention though.

HARRY: I'm sorry, mate... If I'd known that this –

JOE: IT'S NOT FUCKING YOURS RIGHT? GET IT? YOU CAN FORGET ALL ABOUT IT AND KEEP ON FUCKING AROUND LIKE NOTHING MATTERS.

HARRY: Get off me.

JOE: Ruth shouldn't have said anything.

HARRY: She thought I should know.

JOE: Well she should have kept her mouth shut. She should have waited for Mand to say something.

(*A moment*)

HARRY: It won't be mine... But if it was. Just think about that for a minute right...
JOE: Don't need to. It's done.

(*A moment*)

HARRY: She's throwing it all away then... no Uni?
JOE: We'll be fine.
HARRY: Like you said... It's... nothing to do with me... nothing.
JOE: Nothing.

(*Their standoff cools as HARRY turns to go back into the house.*)

FOURTEEN:

MANDY heavily pregnant, cuddling her bump and singing a lullaby. JOE enters but keeps his distance. When MANDY is finished he leaves. A door closes. MANDY turns to look but nothing. MANDY starts to sing again, soft.

FIFTEEN:

MANDY aged 5 with a dolly and pushchair. Playing in her bedroom.

MANDY: That's it lickle girl, go nan-nights now. Shush shush. Mummy tuck you in. That's it. Have sweet dreams lickle girl. You are the best lickle dolly girl everest and tomorrow I'm going to take you to Grand-pa and show him you, because he will be very proud of you. If you sleep ickle girl, sleep, sleep, sleep. And then we can have the ice cream at Grand-pa's because his is bestest. He has the sauces to put on it. Then we can go to the shops with Mama and buy lots of new clothes and shoes and bread. So you need to go nan-nights now because we need our sleeps, yes we do. Yes we do.

(BEN enters with the bin liner, whistling. BEN offers it to MANDY who refuses and runs to a different point in the space – she ages to 16, in a classroom at school.)

We were asked to bring something in that makes us think about our childhood and I've brought this in. She's my dolly – Clarissa – and she went everywhere with me when I was a kid. I used to change her nappy and put her to bed and stuff. I used to cry if my Mum took her off me because she was 'my baby'. I've brought it in today because when I took it to my Granddad's house, my Grand-pa I called him, he would look at her and tell me he was proud of her and ask me what she wanted to be. I would say 'a mummy' like me. He would say 'not an astronaut then? Not doctor or nuclear scientist?' I used to giggle when I was kid... all the words sounded funny and he'd brush his wild grey hair in different directions for each job... As I've got older I've realised... what he was saying. He didn't want the doll to remind me of silly tea parties and pretending to be a Mum. He wanted me to dream bigger than that. I don't think he ever got over Mum not doing more with her life, because she had me... So this doll reminds me of my Grand-pa and how he has inspired me to be the first in our family to do A Levels and go to University. He died last year. I miss him. Thank you.

(*BEN whistles once more and offers the bag. MANDY moves on to a point where her baby is 2yrs old. She wraps the doll up in a blanket and puts it in the pushchair that JOE enters with. The baby is crying*)

	Just take him for a walk Joe, it's the only way he will calm down... he'll drift off if you take it steady.
JOE:	Where am I meant to go?
MANDY:	I don't know Joe but if I don't get a break from that noise I'm going to go mental.
JOE:	Right ok... fucks sake. I'll take him up the park.
MANDY:	No not the park. Just a walk. Make him sleep. He needs sleep. I need sleep.

(*JOE leaves with the baby. BEN whistles once more. MANDY takes a pregnancy test out of her pocket and dumps it into his bag. BEN leaves whistling. MANDY is alone. It is quiet*)

SIXTEEN:

HANNAH in her 20s addresses the audience. In a separate time and place, but sharing the space, BEN is dressed for work on the bins, 20s and addressing a group of workers – represented by the rest of the cast. The dialogue switches between the two moments fluidly.

BEN: So you see it's important that as many of you as possible get involved. We need a good turn out and if voting goes the way we recommend it does... we hope to see those numbers on the picket also.

WORK1: What's the point in striking?

(*Murmur of agreement from the others*)

HANNAH: It's not right is it? I mean all I want to do is send him a get well card. Simple enough. I just want to send a friend a card with a sunset on it... melting in to the... the ground... It looks really warm, but there's frost on the green bits... so you know... it must be cold. It looks positive though. Glowing. It's a get well soon card, he's not been well, apparently. Strange how you still care all these years later isn't it... and it means a lot to me to send this card because Ben has always been there... for me... he's only got a seasonal bug... bugs all

	over the place, no surprise really... I want to send a card and I asked *her* over there... if I could just cut this picture out of a magazine...
WORK1:	What will it achieve? I lose a day's pay and then what? Come back to catch up on the work I didn't do?

(*Further agreement from the others*)

BEN:	I understand your concerns, I do. It's not an easy decision to make to walk out, but that's exactly why it's important to get behind the union and support the action if the ballot goes that way. If we have people crossing the picket then, I agree, it becomes less effective.
WORK2:	What I want to know is why are we striking over pay? I understand the maths of it all but I also understand we're in a better position than most others – we've got jobs for a start. If it was about the job, the things they want us to do, the lack of time given and all that, then I'd be all for it.
HANNAH:	This... A golden sunset... and she gave me these...

(*HANNAH presents some children's safety scissors*)

	It's a joke really isn't it? You can't cut anything with these... but she'd say that's the point... they cut <u>paper</u>...
BEN:	Well you can vote on that basis too – you know we can present whatever... argument we want out there. The national dispute is over pay and pensions, which is important, but if you want to add local conditions to that then I'm all for it.
WORK3:	What's this about that Labour MP coming next week?
BEN:	Officially we don't know that he's coming.
WORK2:	He is though. Got to be. I saw them painting the wagons up the other day.
WORK1:	Fixed the boiler in the canteen as well – only took them 9 months and a 'dignitary'
HANNAH:	That's what they're for... and I know what she's getting at... I know she's seen my arms, in fact she bandaged them the last time... And at my age you don't really want your Mum around putting plasters on things... you're supposed to grow out of that. You're supposed to look after them. And it's not what this is... I just wanted to send a get well soon card... of this sun fading into the horizon. It looks so... beautiful... like you could swim in it...
BEN:	It is annoying, I agree, but at least we're going to be able to present ourselves in the

	best light. That's in our interest as much as it is management.
WORK3:	But he should come and see it how it is.
WORK1:	Labour man should be coming down here to us before boardroom
BEN:	Look I happen to know that he's a union supporter –
WORK2:	Until the papers ask him.

(*Further jeers of support*)

(*HANNAH looks at the picture and the scissors, lost for a moment in her thoughts. HANNAH's phone rings*)

HANNAH: Hello... speaking... well I'm not officially back at work until Monday... I know you could offer the hours to someone else... no I don't want that... It's just that... I know I'm not guaranteed hours... thank you I appreciate that... Really I do appreciate that me being... it has made things more difficult for you... No, look... I'll come in... I'll come in... I'm ok to work, just the doctor said that... but what do Drs know hey? Tomorrow at 8? Yes that fine. I'll be there. I'll be there.

(*HANNAH hangs up the phone, there's a sense that she is going nowhere*)

BEN: When he gets here I'm sure he'll want to speak to you... you know that you can speak to him at any point –

WORK3: When do we get the script?

(*Laughter from the workers*)

BEN: Look let's not... we can focus on that in a few weeks time. Right now it's important that we get the votes in for the ballot, the union recommends a vote for strike action and we can mobilise from there. There's some flyers here if anyone wants to take one away and I'll see you all next –

(*The workers have all shuffled off. BEN takes the flyers in his hand and puts them in the bin liner from before. BEN moves over to HANNAH and takes the scissors carefully from her hands and puts them in the bin. This time he doesn't whistle. BEN ties up the bag and leaves it on the ground. HANNAH gives him the picture, he looks at it and takes HANNAH under his arm as they leave.*)

SEVENTEEN:

A street in summer. HARRY early 20s. 2yrs after the party in TWO. HARRY looks sharp in his suit and shades, confidence oozes from him. MANDY walks the opposite direction down the street, pushing a push chair with a sleeping 2yr old wrapped in it. MANDY looks stressed, she doesn't recognise him.

HARRY: You ignoring me then?
MANDY: (*Turning, tired*) What?

(*HARRY strikes a recognisable pose*)

> H! Hey how are you? Sorry didn't notice –

(*An awkward moment where they're not sure whether or not to embrace*)

HARRY: Its ok shades, suit –
MANDY: And 'we don't see many people dressed like you on Clearview Estate' –
HARRY: (*Defensive*) I never said –
MANDY: I'm winding you up...
HARRY: Right.
MANDY: Too many nights... not enough sleep...
HARRY: I can imagine.

(*Another awkward moment*)

MANDY: You look great. Not seen you round here since –

HARRY: I've been in China... about 18months, working for Dad, buying... well... training.

(*HARRY stops to take her in. MANDY is conscious of this*)

You're looking well yourself there Mand –

RUTH enters a separate area of the stage - in her 30s she addresses the audience holding her notebook from before. RUTH is in a different time and place to HARRY and MANDY. The dialogue switches between the two moments fluidly.

RUTH: I got to my third year at Uni and realised that my plan would only carry me so far. To 21. That's no age really. I'd no idea what to do next. Get a job... that much was obvious... part of the plan, the right thing to do... but... A History degree... Knowing about the role of women in Victorian Britain makes for a great dissertation and empowers you as a woman in all sorts of ways... but it doesn't pay the bills. I don't regret it; don't get me wrong, I loved every second. But I remember coming home for Christmas in that final year and... What next? I read an article online 'Top three jobs most young people today want to do' –

	Famous Actor / Celeb, Famous Musician / Celeb or... teacher... true story.
MANDY:	I look like shit Harry and you know it.
HARRY:	Well you've proven that you <u>can</u> polish a turd then... How's that?
MANDY:	Can't handle all these compliments...

(*Shared laughter, tension easing a little*)

	China? What you doing back?
HARRY:	I'm... moving actually... permanent move out there to understudy one of Dad's buyers.
MANDY:	Hey that's...
HARRY:	(*Blurting it out before he knows he's said* it) I'm marrying his daughter actually... this summer
MANDY:	Congrats... Sounds scary!
HARRY:	A bit... yeah... not as scary as –

(*HARRY points towards the sleeping child*)

RUTH:	I opted for teaching. It's a bit like finding gold coins in the mud... and sometimes, if the kid's got a shit life at home, you find skeletons too... so it's not too far off what I wanted... Pays for the house – new – paid for our wedding too... Pete... Met him on my first placement. Pays for the dogs and holidays and one day it will pay for –

(Cuts herself off, emotional)

	The thing about me and Mandy was that we did everything together.
MANDY:	Oh this little monster... Like his Dad...
HARRY:	Yeah... can see that. Flat out asleep after 10am.
MANDY:	He likes to sleep when it's light... for some reason. He's only just gone off.
HARRY:	Right. How's Joe?
MANDY:	He's...
HARRY:	Yeah.

(A moment)

RUTH: That was our thing... I didn't think she'd go through with it... thought she might... still come to Manchester with me, do all things we'd planned. All the things you should want to do when your 18. All the things you should want to do at 21, 25, 30... Uni, Job, Man, House, Family... <u>that</u> order. That's the order. That's how it's supposed to go. The rewards are obvious, if you do things the right way... Right? Uni, Job, Man, House...
IVF...
Family...

(RUTH composes herself)

(*HARRY stares at the sleeping child, his phones goes off*)

HARRY: Sorry its –
MANDY: I better get him –
HARRY: (*Answering his* phone) Yeah, no that's fine.

(*MANDY is about to leave. HARRY hangs up his phone quickly to keep her there*)

    Just Dad checking up on me. Supposed to be at theirs, going out for a... it's boring really.
MANDY: Enjoy China... the big day... the big move–
HARRY: Can't wait...

(*HARRY's phone again*)

    Sorry.

(*This time HARRY hangs it up straight away*)

    Sorry. Mr Popular today...
MANDY: Nothing changes then?
HARRY: Well... somethings never change...

(*A beat*)

    See you again... say hi to Joe for me?
MANDY: Yeah will do... Bye H. Look after yourself yeah?

HARRY: You too.

(HARRY's phone again, this time he answers it as he walks on. The baby in the pushchair wakes. MANDY puts on her brave face and tries to placate it as she leaves. HARRY stands to watch her go)

RUTH: Still – I'm 'Aunty Ruth' to her kids, when Pete and I visit home and I've real nieces and nephews too. Best thing is you can hand them back... that's what they say... best thing... best laid plans...

(BEN enters whistling and picks up the bin liner from where he left it. He offers it to RUTH. At first she refuses. BEN produces a fresh notepad and pen from his pocket. RUTH gives up the old notepad willingly in exchange for the new. BEN offers the bag to HARRY. HARRY collects together his shades, his wallet and his phone. HARRY hesitates at first before throwing them in. BEN leaves whistling as RUTH opens the new notebook and starts to plan for her future – optimistic. HARRY has a second thought and runs to stop BEN. He reaches into the bag to take out his possessions. He puts his wallet and phone in his pocket before putting the shades on BEN. They all leave)

EIGHTEEN:

JOE, BEN and HARRY drinking at the party – the night before TWO – a conversation they often have and never resolve. MANDY, RUTH and HANNAH are in the toilet, a giant penis has been crudely drawn on the wall behind them. The girls take it in turns to be sat on the toilet/stood talking, changing each time the action cuts to them. They are not as serious as the boys. The dialogue moves between the two areas fluidly.

BEN:	You've got to have something... something you want out of life. What is it you want to do? I know I'm not doing what people expect but it's more important to me to earn some money, move out, get a car, start living a bit. What are your
HARRY/BEN:	(*Patronising*) 'Goals...'
HARRY:	Thank you school careers twat!
BEN:	To the school careers twat!

(*They drink a toast*)

JOE:	(*Confused*) Goals...
HARRY:	He's got goals Bennie Boy – unfortunately they're the kind you find on Fifa '14... but time on his Xbox is building other 'skills'!
JOE:	Leave off it.
HARRY:	When was the last time you sent off a Job application?

(*Cut To: Toilet*)

HANNAH: I wouldn't mind you coming in to our shop after a night out, but you make such a fuss over sauces.
RUTH: (*Drunk, indignant*) You've got to have a condiment on your chips. Right Mand?
HANNAH: Condiment? Who says –
RUTH: Right Mand?
MANDY: Only when you're drunk.
RUTH: (*Looking at the picture of the penis*) Looks like that could do with a condiment on it to keep it safe.

(*They laugh at this. Cut To: Living Room*)

BEN: (*To Harry*) When was the last time you did?
HARRY: This isn't about me... I've a family sock empire to take over. I want to know what he's been doing to get a job?
JOE: CV –
HARRY: That shit they made us do last term of school?
JOE: They said that's what we needed.
HARRY: But no work?

(*Cut To: Toilet*)

RUTH: Best thing about your place Hannah is not the chicken, it's the fried bit.

HANNAH: You mean the skin?
RUTH: No! Not the skin. The fried bit... sits on... it's the fried bit on top of the skin.
HANNAH: That's all you like?
RUTH: That's why we only get one box. I eat the fried bit and the chips.
MANDY: And I eat the chicken.
RUTH: Perfect teamwork.

(*RUTH goes to high-five MANDY but misses and ends up slapping her on the ear*)

MANDY: AH!
RUTH: Oh my God!

(*Cut To: Living Room*)

JOE: Fuck off Harry, you don't know... it's not school where there are people waiting to wipe your arse for you, remind you to do this, hand that in, turn up here at this time... You've no idea what it's like –
HARRY: I know what you're like.
BEN: Oi come on. Keep it civil.
JOE: They don't prepare you for this sort of shit at school. They talk to you about work and stuff, but they don't tell you. Wasting all that time on History when we could have been doing something practical, something like work...

HARRY:	An hour a week of shelf stacking?
JOE:	They didn't give us the full picture
BEN:	Picture of what?
JOE:	Failing. The rejection. Teachers tell you not to do stuff, but fuck all happens if you carry on doing it. I got suspended once, spent a week in bed playing on the Xbox and came back to school no problem. They should have let me fail. Taught me a lesson.
BEN:	Can't do that. Besides... you weren't the worst offender — some didn't come back, not to our school anyway.
HARRY:	Hang on... are you seriously saying that school failed you by not failing you?
JOE:	Yes.

(*Cut To: Toilet*)

RUTH:	Small enough to fit in your clutch?
MANDY:	Not that small no, more like your Mum's handbag?
HANNAH:	Yeah about that big (*HANNAH measures out the size of the micro-pig*)
RUTH:	That red one?
MANDY:	(*Laughing at her*) Whichever! It doesn't matter which bag does it! They're really, really small ok?
HANNAH:	These people on the program had them house trained, like a cat.
RUTH:	Mind. Blown.

(*HANNAH and MANDY enjoy just how drunk RUTH clearly is*)

	Where can I get one?
HANNAH:	You can't take a micro-pig to Uni Ruth!
RUTH:	No but think about it, what if we farmed them? We could have little tiny bacon pieces for breakfast.
MANDY:	You're not taking a micro-pig to Uni –
RUTH:	That's not fair! You're taking a baby!

(*This is the first time HANNAH has heard the news*)

	Oops...
HANNAH:	Who's taking a baby?
RUTH:	Shit. Sorry Mand...

(*Cut To: Living Room*)

HARRY:	That's the most mental thing you've ever come out with.
JOE:	No. It's not.
BEN:	Mate if they did that they'd have written off half our year group.
JOE:	They are written off. Who do you think it is down the jobcentre, on the courses? School kept us ticking over, lying to us – 'you've got potential lad, you just need to settle down' – load of bollocks. I've been

	headed towards this all my life and I'm the only one honest enough to admit it.
BEN:	You just accept that then?
HARRY:	He has to.
BEN:	No he doesn't.
HARRY:	No he's right. What is there for him? Like he said he's good with his hands. So what's he going to do?
BEN:	Go back to the college, it's not too late.
JOE:	No good. Classrooms piss me off. Poxy boxes.
HARRY:	Apprenticeship.
BEN:	Job needs to be there in the first place.
HARRY:	Well then there's only one thing for it – China! That's where all the factory jobs are now. Even Dad is thinking of buying from there.

(*Cut To: Toilet*)

HANNAH:	That's... wow
MANDY:	I was going to say something earlier... just...
HANNAH:	No it's... fine... it's fine... wow... does Joe know?
MANDY:	Yes.
RUTH:	I'm so sorry Mand... I didn't... I think I need to stop drinking these cocktails.
MANDY:	Best idea you've had all night.
HANNAH:	Have you been to the Dr? Checked over –

MANDY: Yeah I told Mum as soon as I found out. She took me straight there.
HANNAH: Well that's good. Oh Mand... a baby?

(*They embrace. RUTH is not well*)

RUTH: I think I need to be...

(*The night starts to get the better of RUTH who is sick*)
(*Cut To: Living Room*)

JOE: There's nothing out there, I've been looking... nothing except wiping old people's arses or calling people up to sell them shit. Fuck that.
BEN: You've got to find something Joe. You've got to.
JOE: Fuck it. Fuck. It.

(*A moment*)

HARRY: his is getting morbid... come on, time to take the piss a bit. I'll get the girls...

(*The scene opens up as HARRY goes calls to the girls in the toilet from the living room*)

    Oi! Ladies! (Suggestive) What can you be doing in there?

(The girls come walking out of the toilet together, RUTH looking like she has just been sick – it's not an attractive sight.)

RUTH: I might have been a little bit sick.

(A moment, before the scene fades)

NINETEEN:

HANNAH working late in the University library, her laptop is open and some books sit sprained and covered in post-it notes beside her. HANNAH has just lost all of her work because of a snapped USB stick.

HANNAH: Shit... no... shit, shit, shit... don't do this to me, no...

(HANNAH fights hard to compose herself. HANNAH's phone rings, she quickly stifles the noise before checking who is calling her at this time. It is BEN who enters another part of the space. Same time, different place. Ben is elated and drunk)

BEN: Hello... Hannah?
HANNAH: Hey Ben... it's me... its late
BEN: Don't you mean early? It's 3 o'clock in the morning.
HANNAH: Really?
BEN: I had to call you
HANNAH: It's not a good time –
BEN: I've been out drinking... student night in town... I'm like one of you!
HANNAH: I'm in the library actually.

(HANNAH fighting back tears)

BEN: I met a boy
HANNAH: A boy?

BEN: Yeah... in the club... I even danced
HANNAH: You must be drunk
BEN: Little bit
HANNAH: I'm sorry Ben but it's not really... I've just lost twelve hours work and the deadline is tomorrow

(*A moment*)

BEN: Are you crying?
HANNAH: A little bit.
BEN: Why?
HANNAH: Nothing really... silly... I've broken my USB, lost all my work.
BEN: That's not good
HANNAH: No?
BEN: That's shit. When's the deadline?
HANNAH: 11:30am tomorrow morning...
BEN: Can't they give you and extenshan... extenshin... extensionion?
HANNAH: No... doesn't quite work like that here... you get one shot.
BEN: Bit like with this boy tonight. One chance to impress
HANNAH: Ben...
BEN: Life is a bit... you know... you only get one shot at it and stuff...

(*A beat*)

	You there?
HANNAH:	Yes I'm here.
BEN:	I just wanted you to know... about the boy... wanted you to be the first to know.
HANNAH:	I'm happy for you
BEN:	I think I'm going to marry him... hey I'm going to take him up the aisle! Haha get it? Up the –
HANNAH:	(*Heated*) BEN! I'd really like to talk but... right now... I'm failing... I'm fucking failing badly and I need to... to do something, pray or something for some miracle because by lunch time tomorrow I might not be a student any more, I might miss my deadline and get booted out... so I'm happy for your new found love and it's great that you thought to ring me first, I'm sure he's... whatever... but I'm...

(*A moment*)

I'm sorry... I shouldn't be taking... you're happy, I'm not... I just...

(*HANNAH fights the tears again, BEN tries to respond as sober as he can*)

BEN: You want me to come over this weekend? I can get a train Friday afternoon after work?

HANNAH:	That would be great but –
BEN:	I'll book tickets then
HANNAH:	No don't... Its fine I'm just being too sensitive really and I've another essay due in next week and I've two shifts at the restaurant so I won't be able to go out or anything even if you do come over.
BEN:	Ok...
HANNAH:	Yeah...

(*A beat*)

BEN:	I better let you go didn't I?
HANNAH:	If you like.
BEN:	Can't keep you up all night... not when you've –
HANNAH:	I don't mind, honest... I'm just... you caught me at the wrong moment...

(*A beat*)

BEN:	When I was talking to this boy I seemed to mention you a lot... got me thinking about missing you... and I suddenly wanted you there... with me and this boy laughing and... stuff...
HANNAH:	Ben...
BEN:	Because you're the best... you're a star you are... the absolute best...
HANNAH:	Thanks Ben

BEN:	No worries. Honest. Any time you need to–
HANNAH:	I know.
BEN:	Night then.
HANNAH:	Night.

(HANNAH fights hard to compose herself, checking the clock she motivates herself to continue)

> 3am... deadline at 11:30am... come on Hannah...

(HANNAH goes back to the laptop to start working, she picks up a few books to flick through them but is clearly tired and finding it hard to make the right decision as to which one to read)

TWENTY:

BEN and JOE aged 12/13 on a playing field, a football sits between them. They've been running from something.

BEN:	You shouldn't have done that
JOE:	Did though
BEN:	You shouldn't have
JOE:	Don't care
BEN:	He's going to kill you when you get in.
JOE:	Fuck him
BEN:	Joe!
JOE:	What? No one here to tell me what to say or do and you're not gonna start either, right?
BEN:	No mate. No...
JOE:	My Dad is a knob. He's not hitting me for that and getting away with it. Wasn't even my fault. He's been in all day, he could have done it. Why's it my job?
BEN:	He's a prick mate. Most of them are.
JOE:	Yeah, he's a bellend!
BEN:	He's a... what?
JOE:	Bellend... (*pointing*) it's that bit on your cock.
BEN:	Ha! Good one.
JOE:	You're not going to get a shag from Hannah if you don't even know what you've got down there.
BEN:	Yeah I do.

JOE:	Bullshit. Teacher's Arse Licker. Bumhole.
BEN:	I'm not.
JOE:	You are. I only ran off because you did. I wanted to see his face... bruise... Then you ran off... You're a great big gaybo.
BEN:	Hey! Shut up.
JOE:	You are though...
BEN:	I'm not.
JOE:	Like round at Harry's the other week, googling all sorts of tits and naked girls... you shout out some singer we never heard of who looks like a man!
BEN:	Piss off. Don't say those words.
JOE:	(*Mocking, immature, like a kid several years younger would*) What words? Gaybo? You big fat gay bumhole?
BEN:	Don't say those... don't say that...

(*BEN moves away upset*)

JOE:	You crying?
BEN:	You shouldn't say that.
JOE:	You crying? Like a big baby?
BEN:	(*At breaking point*) I'M NOT A FUCKING BABY OK?

(*A moment, JOE is taken aback, this is not like BEN*)

JOE:	I was only messing... Ben mate... it's not true so – It's just messing about, no need to

cry about it, it's not bullying or anything so you can't go telling on me either.

(*A moment*)

BEN: I don't like it.
JOE: I get it, alright.
BEN: No... I don't like it when we're round at Harry's looking for... I don't...
JOE: You can't get in trouble if that's what you're scared about. Just stay away from kids and animals and its all ok. Education... teaches you what to do, they should show them in science at school... I'd probably go more if they did.
BEN: It's not that I'm scared of...
JOE: What's your problem then? Scared you'll not be big enough or good enough for Hannah –
BEN: STOP... stop with the Hannah shit right. She's just a friend...
JOE: If you say so.

(*A moment*)

BEN: You remember Sergio?
JOE: Greek kid on the football team, same first name as his second?
BEN: Yeah.
JOE: Good lad, better midfielder than you.

BEN: (*Momentous, blurted out before he changes his mind*) I heard he kissed another lad once.

(*A beat*)

JOE: Who?
BEN: (*Ignoring* him) It was before this family moved away. I heard he was playing on the top pitch and this other lad said goodbye to him and... kissed him.
JOE: Er... Like what Harry did with that girl from Yr9?
BEN: No. Just... on the lips. Nothing too...
JOE: Mate... that's —
BEN: I know.
JOE: Who was it?
BEN: Don't know. I heard from Sergio about it, but he didn't want to grass the other lad up... probably felt a bit embarrassed about it or something.

(*A beat*)

How would you tell someone you did that? Like your parents or mates?
JOE: Probably wouldn't... not in our school, that's why it's not got out yet.

(*A beat – then BEN changing subject a little, lost in his own thoughts*)

BEN: When you hit him today... your Dad... did it feel good?
JOE: At first... Always does when I do it... but... I've got to go back... I'll get ten times worse when I get in.
BEN: I've never hit my Dad. I've wanted to... Too scared to find out what he would do.
JOE: You should try it. Makes you feel bigger.
BEN: He'd kill me... He's too big...

(*The two boys share a moment thinking about what they've got to face at home*)

JOE: Right... You and me mate... I tell you what we're going to do. We're gonna take this ball and try and get it over the fucking sports hall... loser has to buy the McD's on the way home?
BEN: You've never got any money on you!
JOE: I better not lose then.

(*BEN and JOE make their way off the playing field*)

TWENTY-ONE:

HARRY's house the night of the party, everyone in high spirits as HARRY holds court.

HARRY:	And tonight's final award goes to Mr Bean himself –
ALL:	Mr Bean!
HARRY:	Mr Bean himself, our tutor and hero, without him we wouldn't be sat here tonight pissed up and celebrating the end of our exams! Mr Graham might have been a boring –
RUTH:	Bad breathed
BEN:	Brown suited
HANNAH:	Bean!
ALL:	Bean!
HARRY:	But he was <u>our</u> bean
ALL:	Bean!
HARRY:	He was ours and tonight we salute him
ALL:	To Mr Bean!!

(*A shared moment of laughter followed by a mixed response to the cocktail they're drinking*)

HANNAH:	Christ Ruth what's in this?
RUTH:	Secret recipe, can't tell you, would have to kill you after if I did
HARRY:	I think it's nice actually
ALL:	Nice!

MANDY:	You can have mine then, I don't want any more of it.
BEN:	Not like you to turn a drink down Mand?
JOE:	She's not well
HARRY:	Couple more of these and I reckon I won't be well in the morning.
HANNAH:	Slow down a bit then.
HARRY:	Never!
ALL:	Never!
BEN:	What you got planned for us next then H? Alternative School Oscars over with so...
HANNAH:	Let's put some music on for a bit
RUTH:	Yes! Yes! Do that! Now!
BEN:	Not again – we start off alright but then you start shuffling all sorts of crap like YMCA on loop –
ALL:	YMCA! Fun to stay at the YMCA!
JOE:	Shouldn't have said anything mate.
BEN:	Fuck it, do what you like I've got to sleep soon – work in the morning
ALL:	Boo!
HARRY:	Call in sick!
HANNAH:	More hassle than it's worth in my experience.
RUTH:	I'll do it for you. Give me your phone and I'll be all like... 'yeah mother fucker Ben's not coming in yeah cos he like hates his job yeah and thinks you're all wankers so go fuck yourselves yeah?

(*A moment of quiet shock at this outburst*)

MANDY: How many of those cocktails you had Ruth?

RUTH: I'm not sure... I think I'm going to be...

(*RUTH runs out into the kitchen, followed by HARRY*)

HARRY: (*As he's going* off) Not again! Not the floor Ruth, not the floor! Get it in something, the bin or... this do it in these!

HANNAH: I should check on that, but I'm not going to...

BEN: You're right you know Joe.

JOE: Thanks. Don't know what I'm right about but thanks.

BEN: I do hate my fucking job. I work with a right bunch of pricks. They do nothing but piss me about because I'm the youngest. Trying to send me for buckets of steam and... other stupid shit... they don't get it that I've got a brain. Just think I'm being mardy if I don't play along.

JOE: Fuck 'em then mate

BEN: Yeah fuck 'em

HANNAH: Ben –

BEN: You know what I'm going to throw my uniform in the bin tonight, keep drinking with you lot and in the morning I'm going tell them to stuff it.

HANNAH: Think about this Ben, you don't want to do this.
MANDY: Don't Ben...
JOE: Leave him! Go on Ben!
BEN: I only work there because of him... Fuck him... fuck him and his... ways...
JOE: (*Laughing*) Ways?
BEN: Excuse me...

(*BEN grabs his bag from the side of the sofa, he takes out his clothes and marches off through the Kitchen as HARRY returns dragging a weary RUTH, he places her on the floor – in the position we find her in TWO*)

HANNAH: Is Ruth alright?
HARRY: She didn't get it on the floor... that's the important part.
MANDY: Told you to lay off the cocktails... she throws anything in.
HARRY: Secret Recipe.

(*BEN re-enters shirtless as in TWO*)

HARRY: Ha! Strippers here!
BEN: I did it.
JOE: Awesome
HARRY: Did what?
BEN: I threw off the chains of employment!
HARRY: What?
MANDY: He's thrown his work clothes away

HANNAH:	Why Ben? And why have you thrown your own shirt off as well?
BEN:	Got carried away in the moment.
HARRY:	Yes mate... that's what I'm talking about.
HANNAH:	He doesn't need advice from you
BEN:	I do actually. From now on you're my careers advisor twat
ALL:	Careers Twat!
HARRY:	It would be an honour mate... right let's get you sorted.

(*HARRY grabs a marker pen, takes a picture of the wall*)

	Now any careers twat will tell you –
ALL:	Careers twat!
HARRY:	(*Impersonating their careers advisor*) Settle down class. Now it's important that you have a plan young Bennie boy... important to sit and work it out. What you want to do, where you want to go etc. So... where do you see yourself in five years time?

(*At this HARRY starts to write BEN's name on the wall and draws a line to represent five years*)

ALL:	No! Harry! You fucking idiot!
BEN:	In five year's time? I'll Prime Minister!

(*They all laugh at this and the party continues. HARRY writes up Prime Minister at the end of the line and the scene fades*)

TWENTY-TWO:

Everyone takes their positions as in ONE. JOE is with the pushchair.

JOE:	Terrified... if I'm honest. Fuck all we can do now though is there. You just get up and another day starts.
HARRY:	We all have a reason for getting out of bed in a morning. For some it's what you can spend the money on after.
BEN:	Others it's a matter of principles –
HANNAH:	Or a desire to keep busy.
RUTH:	Because you're trying to build a future... something better...
MANDY:	Or just to put food on the table... today...
JOE:	I don't understand. I might be too far gone.
HARRY:	You never started mate.
RUTH:	What about him?
JOE:	My boy?
MANDY:	Our son.
JOE:	Daniel.
RUTH:	Isn't he enough? What would you do for him?
JOE:	Anything.
HANNAH:	Do it then.
ALL:	Change things.

(*Everyone is still as JOE speaks to his son*)

JOE: You're tiny. Smaller than I thought you'd be. Pink and blue... like you've been pinched all over. Your body looks like my legs used to when my Dad... your Granddad... used to slap us. Hard. Sometimes I deserved it – I can be a right pri... (*correcting* himself) idiot, I know that – but most of the time it was just his way... you know. I tried to impress him when I was a kid. I'd follow him out into the back yard to tidy things up, move bricks, grab weeds, whatever... But there was always something. Too cold. Too dirty. Too heavy. I think I was just working it out, but he didn't have time for that. Crack! Ears burning and I'm back in the house watching through the window. 'Weak backed bleeder'. But that was only work <u>he</u> ever did. Used to claim for all of us. Mum on disability, he was her carer, more kids than they could look after but the money came in so it was alright...

(*JOE leans down to take the baby from the pushchair, he holds it in his arms*)

At school they talked about role-models, when I was in detention or getting a bollocking (*Stopping*) sorry, getting told off... I used to say my Dad because we had the biggest TV on our street and he never worked a day. Because that's all that mattered then. What TV, what trainers, what phone, what shirt, what chain... They used to talk about us at school, that's why I got into trouble, usually because I'd smacked someone in the mouth for slagging off my Mum and Dad – stood up for him even though he was a bastard (*Stopping*) sorry... that's best word him. Made me feel like I wasn't worth much and I guess I'm not. Not worth employing at any rate hey?

(*JOE holds the baby in tight*)

You're not rubbish at all, you're not thick as shit, too weak to work, too stupid to get on... You'll be none of those things, not to me. I've made a lot of mistakes son, but you... you're the best of the lot. Honest. Honest to fucking God. And I'm going to try. Harder. I am. I going to...

Blackout

END